Butcher,
Baker,
Epigram Maker

ALSO BY MICHAEL BRAUDE

Who's Zoo

The First 30 Odd Years: An Autobiography

A Question of Identity

Village Vignettes

BUTCHER,
BAKER,
EPIGRAM MAKER

by Michael Braude

Illustrated by *New Yorker* artist Mischa Richter

Macmillan Publishing Company
New York

Collier Macmillan Publishers
London

Macmillan Publishing Company
866 Third Avenue, New York, N.Y. 10022
Collier Macmillan Canada, Inc.

Library of Congress Cataloging in Publication Data

Braude, Michael.
  Butcher, baker, epigram maker.

  1. Epigrams.   I. Title.
PS3552.R34B8   1984   818'.5402   84-9660
  ISBN 0-02-514610-6

10 9 8 7 6 5 4 3 2 1

Designed by Jack Meserole

Printed in the United States of America

To Lillian, Judi, Adam and Rachel Frayda

Contents

Butcher,
Baker,
Epigram Maker

Anon

He cloaked his true identity,
determined to remain unnamed:
His motive?—Was it modesty?
Or did he simply feel ashamed?

Did his good wife dislike the poem,
think little of him as a writer?
Would it have broken up their home
if she discovered he defied her?

What was his calling, trade or craft?
Could he have been a pastry cook?
Would any of his friends have laughed
had it come out he wrote a book?

No consequence without a cause—
that's why one safely can assume:
the reason he's anonymous,
he could not find a *nom de plume*.

Abelard and Eloise

Their shocking dalliance
upset medieval France,
and down to our own day
one still hears Frenchmen say:

Because he was her tutor
he should not have pursued her;
to carry on with pupils
betrays a lack of scruples.

As one of his best students
she should have practiced prudence,
and scolded the professor
each time he would caress her.

But there are those who claim
the *times* deserve the blame:
In ages dark and middle
what's there to do but diddle?

Abraham

His mother tucks him in the pram
and proudly wheels him through the park,
where she shows off young Abraham,
her son the patriarch.

And to perpetuate the line,
she nightly prays before the arc
that he will spurn a concubine
and wed a matriarch.

Alexander

In all my life I never won
impressive sobriquets like "Great":
what worries me is when I'm gone
will I, at least, be called "the late"?

Alexander

B

Beatrice and Dante

Was it your family or self
that turned you so fiercely anti?
Could it have been your being Guelph
or overly *pedante*?
Admittedly a Ghibelline,
but this is only half the story—
the fact is that she was a teen
which also made it statutory.

Blake

Tigers do not burn bright
in the forest of the night:
If they did, one might conclude
that they were being barbecued.

Boccaccio

When pestilence sweeps through the city of Rome
a nobleman asks every friend to his home
and clinically studies the view he espouses
that plagues very seldom attack both your houses.

4

Buddha

While Moses scales Mount Sinai's crest
Jehovah to be near,
his counterpart, preferring rest,
keeps squatting on his rear.

While Jesus gives up life that peace
may reign forever more,
Gautama, flabby and obese,
does not stir from the floor.

Is this dichotomy well founded
or just another Christian bias
against a prophet who'd been grounded
and never left his dais?

C

Lewis Carroll

She looked around the room
and then from side to side;
"Where is the guinea pig?"
a tearful Alice cried.

"He did not come to tea,"
she heard the rabbit answer,
"because he's in the lab
researching liver cancer."

"That's not what I had heard,"
the walrus said protesting,
"it's polio and syphilis
the guinea pig is testing."

"A bold and flagrant lie,"
the hatter fulminated.
"In truth the guinea pig
is being vaccinated."

"Emphatically not so,"
the tortoise interjected,
"the guinea pig, in fact,
is being vivisected."

"I'm desolate with grief,"
said Alice in lament,
"he should have come to tea
and not experiment."

Charon

Should his ferry stray on rocks,
passengers need not feel nervous;
for he carries ample stocks
of the finest death preservers.

Chatterley

Your game is beautiful this year,
the vixen never looked more trim—
your keeper is superb, we hear,
our wives would like to borrow him.

D

Damon   and   Pythias

Neglected, spurned, out of
  sorts,
his wife grew more and
  more despondent,
until she took him to the
  courts
and named the friend
  as . . .   co-respondent.

Daniel

That time when God heard lions roar
and then, a man's heartrending prayer,
He vacillated at length before
deciding which of them to spare.

Darwin

At odds with Genesis,
he tells me I've evolved;
whate'er my background is,
the problem's still unsolved.

The question is not who
my forebears may have been,
but rather what I do
with a delinquent teen,

Darwin

Whose single saving trait,
his only contribution,
has been to escalate
the counter-evolution.

David

Courageous and defiant,
no older than a teen,
the boy approached the giant,
that loathsome Philistine.

He found a jagged stone
to put inside his sling,
and after it was thrown
the Hebrews crowned him king.

So parents should be glad
instead of having qualms—
however wild their lad,
he'll soon be writing psalms.

Diogenes

Assuming that he found it,
would he have cried "Eureka!"
or thrown a veil around it,
again become the seeker?

Dostoyevsky

The Marxes all had brothers, too,
as did each Ringling, Wright, and Smith:
so why this long drawn out to do
on Karamazov's kin and kith?

Einstein

E

Einstein

$$\frac{\text{Man} + \text{Man}}{\text{Borders}} = \text{War}$$

This bold equation proves
his theory was right,
that darkness always moves
at twice the speed of light.

T. S. Eliot

Dare he eat a peach—
and what about a pear?
Rhetorical or not,
his question was not fair.

Did Eliot forget—
or was he inastute—
to overlook the prevalence
of allergies to fruit?

Euclid

There is a ratio called pi;
and parallels will never meet.
Geometricians do not die;
they just displace six cubic feet.

F

Ferdinand

The first time that seafaring fella
petitioned you for a flotilla,
you dismissed him as crazy,
befuddled and hazy;
but what did you tell Isabella?

The next time that Christopher came
you already knew him by name;
you still must have laughed,
considered him daft;
but did your good wife feel the same?

What probably happened was that
the pair had engaged in a spat;
and if Isabella
had not backed that fella,
we'd still think the world was flat.

Fermi

A bevy of drakes and a duck
ran into a spate of bad luck
while winging their way
across Hudson Bay
from Memphis to Vladivostok.

A red border guard in Kamchatka
had drunk one too many a vodka,
flashed Moscow the news
of raiding U-2s,
and turned the cold war into hotka.

Fermi

He triggered a hydrogen rocket,
it lofted but hit an air pocket,
went sharply off course,
continued full force,
exploding in far-off Woonsocket.

When Washington, Paris and Bonn
discovered what Russia had done,
they notified SAC
to launch an attack
and use every last megaton.

The upshot of this whole affair—
the ducks had to stay in the air,
for Vladivostok
at seven o'clock
had vanished, was no longer there.

This story, of course, has a crux,
our status is one of great flux,
and based on all trends
our fine feathered friends
will end up being dead ducks.

Ford Madox Ford

Had he been just a bit more game
and not afraid of the untoward,
he might have changed his middle name
and faced the world as Ford Ford Ford.

G

David Garrick

A native with guide books and maps
came close to a nervous collapse
when he saw the grave
of play-acting Dave
in Westminster's storied old apse.

In contrast, a stage-stricken foreigner
emoted no less than a mourner,
cried out with a tear
the bards that lie here
have trespassed this Thespian's corner.

Granddaughter-Goose

Baa, baa, black sheep,
And what were your deeds this fine day?
"Forged a few checks,
had me some sex,
then whisked off to my hideaway."

Baa, baa, black sheep,
And what did you do in between?
"Burgled a shop,
beat up a cop,
then had me a shot of morphine."

Baa, baa, black sheep,
And what do you have in the mill?
"Steal the crown jewels,
break all the rules
then afterward read Fanny Hill."

Thomas Gray

The village churchyard that you celebrated—
uncared for, overgrown with weeds, neglected,
by space sequestered, history outdated—
no wonder that it made you feel dejected.

If you had gone to Forest Lawn, not here,
beheld the air foam mattress, double spring,
the TV set that stands beside each bier,
you would have said, "Ah, death, where is thy sting?"

The Brothers Grimm

The fairy tales they told
to children young in years,
are much too frank and bold
for tender adult ears.

Edgar Guest

The strophes you were wont to write
were rarely rated with the best:
prosaic, homespun, often trite—
but still, dear Edgar, be my guest.

I'll keep you in the attic hall
surrounded by the things I cherish—
old Grandpa's cane, Aunt Maggie's shawl,
that lithograph by Maxfield Parrish.

These treasured souvenirs are great
for ridding human hearts of malice:
but since you were no laureate,
I think I'll stick with digitalis.

Homer

H

Heinrich Heine

Your poetry was burned
because you were a Jew;
if you had been more current,
they would have burned you.

Homer

The number of cities at one time was seven
and each one claimed credit for giving him birth,
but recently Texas has made it eleven
with Dallas, Port Arthur, Laredo, Fort Worth.

The opulent, nouveau riche cities of grease
aggressively pressing their claim to the kudos,
ascribed by none other than brave Hercules
to Colophon, Smyrna, Salamis or Argos.

The Russians now also have entered the list
with fervor that comes very close to hysteria—
the Marxist professors all stoutly insist
that Homer was probably reared in Siberia.

This issue of where the great poet was born
ranks high among history's puzzling conundrums:
the scholars who ask was he native or foreign
have oftentimes wished that the Greeks had used
    condoms.

Robin Hood

His place in history secure,
and yet not free from some suspicion—
he robbed the rich to help the poor,
but did he charge a slight commission?

Washington Irving

Some students have been known to wonder
if Rip Van Winkle was unique;
they claim that Irving put his readers under.
They didn't waken for a week.

Isaiah

Was it not you who promised us
that lions would lie down with lambs?
Were you, one wonders, serious,
or merely coining epigrams?

Was it not you who prophesied
that plowshares would be made of swords?
It's time that you forgot your pride
and started eating all those words.

Ivan the Terrible

His name, devoid of tact,
embarrasses and shocks us:
Still, how would we react
to Ivan the Obnoxious?

J

Job

Stripped of pious exegetics,
the plain and unadorned fact is,
when prayers failed as had the medics,
he sued Jehovah for malpractice.

Joseph

As all of us have heard,
one day the Cairo bourse
saw common and preferred
sustain a sharp reverse.

The analysts detected
few grounds for any fears:
the last thing they expected
were seven famine years.

But something went awry—
a credit crunch, perhaps—
and from an all-time high
to virtual collapse.

The blue-chip pyramids,
both north and on the Delta
elicited no bids
with no one left to sell to.

The House of Rameses,
none more conservative,
dumped all securities
in order to survive.

Despairing, Nefertiti
hastened to the sphinx:
the oracle took pity,
said, "Go and sell your minks."

An ancestor of Mark's
and Caesar's future mistress,
reduced to sleep in parks
and cadge for drinks in bistros.

A financier in Pithom,
accused and brought to trial—
he could not take it with him
and so jumped in the Nile.

The Brothers Tutankhamen,
their backs against the wall,
sold every share of common
to meet a margin call.

Why even Pharaoh's court
grew fearful of the risks
and started going short
on Luxor obelisks.

An economic crisis
engulfing rich and poor,
investors prayed to Isis
or Joseph for a cure.

Though Joseph had full sway,
the indices hit bottom
and many moved away
to Gomorrah and Sodom.

And there they played the market—
at least, so one supposes—
between the patriarchate
and Exodus of Moses.

The moral of this story,
by no means hard to find—
investors won't be sorry
if they but keep in mind:

Except for Kuhn & Loeb,
all others should recall
the references in Job
to streets called Wailing Wall.

Joshua

Joshua

No general of woman born
approached his feat at Jericho;
he felled each rampart with his horn—
of course, he played fortissimo.

K

Keats

If silent music is preferred
and songs are sweeter when unheard,
it follows odes will only please
if left inside parentheses.

Martin Luther King

Named for a man who dared berate
an ancient dogma and its rites,
he went on to extrapolate
the fallibility of whites.

and Martin Luther

An Aryan much prone to schism,
it safely can be postulated
he would have scored black plagiarism
that had his name desegregated.

L

Charles Lamb

The author regarded by all as a prig
exclaimed after tasting roast pig,
"For succulent lamb
I don't give a damn—
Forgive me, I meant to say, fig."

Livy

Historically anti-Semitic,
this Roman must have been a hero
to keep a Jewish patronymic
and not assume a name like Nero.

Longfellow

Life, he wrote, was earnest, real,
and the grave was not its due—
so on his death's centennial
one questions if he's changed his view.

Louis XVI

"I'd like a piece of cake, my pet,"
the sixteenth Louis said.
"We're out of cake," snapped Antoinette,
"why don't you eat some bread?"

On hearing her the king exploded,
"In faith, you are a fiend;
besides, I'm sure you'll be misquoted
and have us guillotined."

M

Malory

As ye gather round the table,
knights in armor, dames in sable,
first salute the king, none other,
shouting loudly, Arthur, Arthur.
Now relaxed within your chairs,
listen to the minstrel's airs
as he sings of Launcelot,
bravest knight in Camelot,
who, in quest of Holy Grail,
did not eschew a single trail.
Replete with perils boldly faced,
just to keep all women chaste.
Now allow your eyes to droop
downward to the bowls of soup
which the lackeys will deliver
after the chopped griffin liver,
pickled innards, kidneywurst,
all designed to raise a thirst.
Appetizers finger-lickin'
heralding the roasted chicken
sure to please you so much more
than sautéed or broiled boar:
no side dishes, none at all,
nothing but cholesterol.
Use your fingers, don't resent it,
forks have not yet been invented.
Should you slobber as you dunk,
wipe your lips off on the monk—
matchless napkin the attire
of a chaste, God-fearing friar.
If he starts to make a fuss,
jog his memory with Brother Huss,

Malory

Wycliffe or the Albigensians
stirring up religious tensions.
Now you reach the time at last
near the end of the repast:
try avoiding the mistake
of ordering a piece of cake—
if you won't start eating fruit,
you'll outgrow that armor suit.
With the final calorie
once again comes Malory.
As ye rise up from the table,
knights in armor, dames in sable,
bow before him and no other
shouting loudly, Author! Author!
If you promise not to laugh,
you may get his autograph.

Mary and Her Lamb

She sent the lamb to school one day
but all it did was sleep,
and Mary, who had gone along,
received a fellowsheep.

The ovine had a little pet
it christened Mary Human,
who couldn't learn any tricks
because it lacked acumen.

Molière

If he had been writing today,
reviewers would probably say:
"The *mots* of great wits
do not assure hits,
not even off Champs Élysées."

Moses

A story not apt to inspire us
was found on an ancient papyrus—
it seems that when Moses
came down with sclerosis,
he prayed not to God but Osiris.

N

Ogden Nash

Few flights of fancy,
his muse a scold
the rhythms chancy—
if truth be told.

Yet after all
is said and done,
his doggerel
transcends mere fun.

He took his time
but in the end
found proper rhyme
although the quest might take him from Poughkeepsie
    to South Bend.

And on the day
of his demise
his friends did say
with tearful eyes:

"Your *mot* was *juste,*
oh, Ogden Nash . . .
but dust to dust
and Nash to ash."

Newton

Eve ate the apple, pits and all
which is the reason for the Fall,
but not till Isaac was to tell
were we to learn why apples fell.

Nobel

You're lavish with your riches
to scientists renowned;
yet writers of pastiches
you've virtually disowned.

You've given huge bonanzas
to novelist and scholar;
but author of light stanzas
has yet to see a dollar.

The dynamite, you know, sir,
shows very little bias;
but doggerel composers
you've treated like pariahs.

It's clear that you've forgotten
that famed Shakespearean verse—
though Denmark may be rotten,
in Sweden it's much worse.

Eugene O'Neill

O

Eugene O'Neill

I, too, have had desires
but not beneath the elms;
the spark that kindles fires
I find in different realms:

A Botticelli bust,
a sip of Burgundy.
It's this that whets my lust,
and not a chestnut tree.

A softly lighted bar,
a dancing chorus line,
the twang of a guitar
but not a brooding pine.

I've had my interludes,
not quite as strange as others:
I've had my share of nudes
though very few stepmothers.

Ophelia

She fell in love with him,
still Hamlet did resist her—
so she went for a swim,
did not become a sister.

Orwell

Nineteen Hundred, Eighty-Four
is no longer by and by . . .
Brother Big resides next door
and runs the FBI.

P

Pandora

The maiden had a change of heart,
when she recovered from the shock;
she blamed the gods, at least, in part
for having used a flimsy lock.

Dorothy Parker

The Thirties, quarantined by history,
a decade enclaved, set apart in time,
defined and annotated by the plea—
I'm hungry, mister, can you spare a dime?

Impaled by memories of war that was,
forebodings of another still to come,
and in between a catatonic pause
to mark the tryst between the to and from.

And that is when you took the stage, Miss Parker,
to save a darkened world from growing darker.

Walter Pater

There'd been no filius
if Walter Pater's pater
did not have any use
for Walter Pater's mater.

Picasso

The critics have been troubled by
his underlying attitudes
towards human physiognomy
as manifested in his nudes.

The nostrils dangle from the thighs,
a forehead lurks inside the mouth;
instead of two, he paints three eyes
one looking north, the others south.

The profile is disoriented,
chin is where the spine should be:
an Adam's apple is indented
and nestles just below the knee.

The ears resemble scimitars
and there's no sign of any nose—
small wonder people thank their stars
they never had been asked to pose.

Plato

No thinker more observant,
his legacy ironic—
a love however fervent,
but nonetheless platonic.

This substitute for sex
has never overjoyed us—
cerebral and complex,
it can't compare with coitus.

Edgar Allan Poe

When quoth the raven "Nevermore,"
perhaps the bard of Baltimore
had uttered a mere metaphor.

There is one scholar who thinks not:
he claims the raven smoked a lot
and guzzled whiskey like a sot.

His theory suggests, of course,
that those repeated "nevermores"
conveyed the raven's deep remorse.

Edgar Allan Poe

True or not, we'll never know.
The life of Edgar Allan Poe
was often marked by eating crow.

Alexander Pope

His couplets were sparkling and witty,
sententious, concise, debonair—
that's why all the greater the pity
he wrote no third line for a spare.

Ezra Pound

Let us reroute our errant thoughts
from trivia to matters now profound.
And then, our minds honed razor-sharp,
we're ready to devour the flesh of Pound.

Q

Quiller-Couch

When young, I thought him humorous,
nor have I changed my mind—
although by now he's posthumous
and I'm not far behind.

Quintilian

Though you are held in great esteem, Quintilian,
I'll never read your celebrated tract:
not even if I live to be a million
and someone thought to have you paperbacked.

Quisling

When he bid welcome the invader
and raised his voice to shout *"Sieg heil,"*
some branded him as the archtraitor,
while others called him imbecile.

Which of these views is true or false—
a question even time can't settle—
gone the brute Neanderthals
but also gone the *shtetel*.

R

Rabelais

Oh, Rabelais, oh, Rabelais
was there a critic in your day
who was indignant and dismayed
because you called a spade a spade?

Did he regard your prose unfit
and try to disembellish it;
did he insist you be deterred
from using the four-letter word?

Oh, Rabelais, oh, Rabelais,
regardless of what critics say,
but for your purple metaphors,
we'd still be saying intercourse.

For when it comes to venery,
none other than Pat Hen-e-ry
asserted with his dying breath,
"Give me pornography or death."

Rasputin

When word of the slaying reached Nicholas,
he dismissed the report as ridiculous,
but all of his nieces
cried, falling to pieces,
"Now who is there left who will tickle us?"

James Whitcomb Riley

The critics will often imply
his poetry leaves them a bit numb:
but no one can ever deny
that he lived the life of James Whitcomb.

43

Rabelais

S

Samson

She clipped his hair
from here to there—
her aim to make him neuter.
But who can say
she had her way
since he remained hirsuter.

Sappho

Had someone attempted to curb her,
she might not have pointed the way
to Dickinson, Brontë and Ferber,
George Eliot, Edna Millay.

A woman need no longer knit well
nor leave the arts strictly alone—
this holds for Rossetti and Sitwell,
Elizabeths Browning and Bowen.

Shakespeare

Will Shakespeare, it's claimed, was a fellow
who wasn't outstandingly bright
and could not have written *Othello,*
the Sonnets or even *Twelfth Night.*

Among English scholars, et cetera,
the question this raises is who
wrote *Antony and Cleopatra,*
The Merchant of Venice, and *Shrew.*

If Marlowe, as is often reckoned,
in fact penned each line and each word,
one wonders if Edward is second
and what befell Richard at third.

The Bacon support, 'twould appear,
is spirited in the extreme,
they not only give him *King Lear*
but also *Midsummer Night's Dream*.

This argument's still in full swing
and were I allowed to take part,
I'd stress that the play is the thing,
to quote Messrs. Rodgers and Hart.

Shaw

Those prefaces
by G.B.S.—
let no one be misled—
their purpose was
to win applause
before a line was said.

Socrates

(A DIALOGUE AT THE TRIAL)

Prosecutor:
Were you subversive, as was said?
Did you traduce our cherished youth?
Some testified you are a red,
this court expects you'll tell the truth.

Socrates:
I never read *Das Kapital,*
The New Republic or *The Nation,*
I don't believe in Marx at all
or artificial fluoridation.

Shaw

Prosecutor:
I will not tolerate such wiles
in disavowing anarchism—
each one of your so-called denials
involved a sheer anachronism . . .

Socrates:
We are in dreadful jeopardy,
we teeter-totter on the brink,
and this is all you'll hear from me—
now, kindly let me have that drink.

Prosecutor:
This last remark you'll surely rue,
or was it meant to be a joke?
The hemlock is an alien brew,
a patriot drinks only Coke!!

Solomon

What happened in the ladies' wing
that made you so depressed and feckless—
did Ruth demand a sapphire ring
and Jezebel a diamond necklace?

Did Hepzibah insinuate
she was in need of a new tunic,
and Magdalene bemoan her fate
unable to seduce her eunuch?

Was Shulamith dissatisfied
with romance in a crowded harem;
did she object to each new bride
as just one more who'd have to share him?

And what about sweet Deborah,
was she unhappy with her lot?
Did Lillith clamor for a bra
and Sheba for a single cot?

48

Solomon

From all that's written and been said,
there's truly much to give one pause—
a harem with a thousand head
has just as many mother-in-laws.

Soothsayers

Do not beware the Ides
though seers may be offended;
whatever else abides,
the winter snows have ended.

Yes, spring is on the way
on equinoctial tides,
ignore what soothsayers say
and welcome March's Ides.

Sophocles

What was that complex called
before you wrote that drama?
Precisely who's at fault ·
when a daughter hates her mama?

Swift

The Lilliputians weren't small,
the Dean was misapprised.
It's Gulliver who was too tall
and grossly oversized.

T

Teller

So when the bomb evolves
from *A* to *U*
to sound the drama's final cue;
and when an apple falls too soon—
not down but up, lands on the moon—
the time has come to beat the drum,
make *V* signs with your toe and thumb
and march across irradiated ground
while waving banners all around. . . .
Yes, be prepared to don gas masks
and other funerary tasks!
Irkutsk lies buried in debris,
New York seeks safety in the sea,
and not a daisy blooms to fashion wreaths
for those who die grim alphabetic deaths,
and join the doomsday pantomime
unraveling within the sepulcher of time.

Thoreau

In Walden, Henry, we've had changes,
the world won't stand still, you know:
your town now has two driving ranges,
an outdoor moving picture show.

Filene's is there and Macy's, too,
Helena Rubinstein and Murray's;
a dime store, Saks Fifth Avenue,
a restaurant that features curries.

Thoreau

A launderette and three boutiques,
a Congregationalist church,
the brokers, Hornblower-Weeks,
ten charter members of John Birch.

Five analysts, a private school,
an FM station, used car row,
a new motel with swimming pool . . .
and that's the way it goes, Thoreau.

So now you know, come glory day
and everyone who died is called on,
you'd better practice saying "nay"
for you won't like it now at Walden.

Tolstoy

The war in *War and Peace* is cold,
Karenina is gray and old.
No wonder readers now are switchin'
to Aleksandr Solzhenitsyn.

U

The Underground

No roll call of the underground
but mentions Maquis, Czechs and Poles.
It's strange, indeed, that I never found
a single reference to moles.

Untermeyer

Anthologist par excellence
and yet not error-free.
How else explain the circumstance,
he always slighted me.

V

Villon

It's said he cheated, ravaged, stole,
and that he wrote a graceful rhyme.
I cannot tell, upon my soul,
which may have been his greater crime.

Virgil

Bleed-ins at Kent, freedom songs,
ambushes by Viet Congs,
paddies where rice will not grow—
arma virumque cano!

Flame throwers, napalm at dusk,
Johnson, Westmoreland and Rusk
frustrated by Comrade Ho—
arma virumque cano!

Body counts, defoliation,
a Buddhist monk's self-immolation,
soldier graves, row upon row—
arma virumque cano!

And let us not ever forget
the carnage referred to as Tet;
it happened not too long ago—
arma virumque cano!

Protests on Washington streets,
joy over news of defeats,
rioting in Chicago—
arma virumque cano!

And now that the war is behind us,
let Virgil's *Aeneid* remind us
the script has changed little since Troy—
arma virumque Hanoi!

Wilde

Rebecca West

It seems that when Rebecca
had come to visit Mecca,
she said triumphantly:
"At last, the East meets me."

Wilde

If Oscar was wild,
was Thornton Wilder?
If Oscar was witty,
was John Greenleaf Whittier?
And if Oscar was male,
is Norman Mailer?

X

Xanthippe

Did he make love to you in bed
as any normal husband might,
or did he like to talk instead,
philosophize throughout the night?

The time that you were still a bride,
did he enthuse or was he glum
because he was preoccupied
developing an axiom?

Did he prefer to be with men,
and was he difficult to please?
If you were told to choose again,
would you still marry Socrates?

Xavier

When Xavier set sail for Ind.,
he was in a prodigious hurry
to save the heathens who had sinned
and taste the native rice and curry.

With burning missionary zeal
he'd preach the gospel of the Cross;
then sit down to a tempting meal
of curried lamb with chutney sauce.

They called him saint for all his labors
in dark, benighted Hindustan;
but to his friends and next-door neighbors
he always was the trencherman.

And when the godly man expired
and stood at heaven's golden gates,
he turned to Peter and inquired
if rice and curry transmigrates.

Xenophon

He loathed the Asian foe
and said so in his books,
yet never stooped so low
as to call the Persians gooks.

Y

Yevtushenko

He hails the goals in every Five Year Plan,
salutes each Soviet victory in space,
provided that the Kremlin says he can:
If not, he's ready to erase.

Z

Zeno

It's you who warned Stoics
that nothing will prevail.
Regardless of heroics,
unhappy ends each tale.

Zenobia

Palmyra's queen, archepicene—
the words of her maligners;
delinquency, the legacy,
she willed to Asian Minors.

Seduced her cousins by the dozens,
and when their numbers slipped,
took up with brothers or any others
sufficiently equipped.

Promiscuous and sensuous,
not given to remorse:
It's been implied she even tried
romancing with a horse.

But rue the day, the steed said "neigh,"
refused the role of satyr.
Still Russia's queen, Great Catherine,
would try to emulate her.

So now we see that history
is apt to replicate
Zenobia's weird phobias
or Nixon's Watergate.

A precedent for each event,
the syllogists might say
that matrimony of maid and pony
may not be far away.

Zenobia

King Zog

Who was it lost a bloody war,
did not get on with paramour,
mislaid the key to palace door,
addressed the court in metaphor,
and left his hearers unagog?
His Royal Majesty, King Zog.

Who was it hanged in effigy,
had arsenic put in his tea,
was never dandled on a knee
and suffered such anxiety
he never did sleep like a log?
His Royal Majesty, King Zog.

Who was it had a scheming heir,
a daughter cruel and unfair,
advisers who were never there
and so much worry, so much care
they always called him "underdog"?
His Royal Majesty, King Zog.

Zola

Without the Dreyfuses in prison,
there'd be no books like *J'Accuse,*
and without anti-Semitism
there probably would be no Jews.

Epilogue

And now, alas, the time has come
to take our leave from you, dear reader—
our parting gift, a tidy sum
of iambs, metaphors and meter.

And just by way of extra measure,
a veritable Who Is Who,
which earnestly it's hoped you'll treasure;
after this, our fond adieu.

The list is skimpy, we admit,
with plethoras of missing names—
no references to William Pitt,
Descartes, Spinoza, Henry James.

Confucius, Whitman, Thomas Mann:
Erasmus, too, has been forgotten,
along with Bellow, Kublai Khan,
Aquinas, Bach, and Lord Mountbatten.

This may raise questions, scarcely new,
among them, what are the criteria
for being named in Who's Who
of England, France or Siberia.

Wealth, for one, and family,
a good Park Avenue address;
a box at every symphony
and frequent mention in the press.

Now, most of us won't qualify
and, sad to say, we're not a few;
our compensation, when we die,
at least, we'll make Who Wasn't Who.

But we're convinced the rumor's true,
that fickle and short-lived is fame,
as witnessed by the fact Who's Who
has never listed What's-His-Name.